A Father's Cry

MICHAEL R. BURSE JR.

Fulton Books, Inc.
Meadville, PA

Published by Fulton Books 2021

ISBN 978-1-63985-220-8 (paperback)
ISBN 978-1-63985-221-5 (digital)

Printed in the United States of America

Dedicated to my sister Lasonya R. Burse, who passed away on June 27, 2020, at 05:05 a.m. I wrote this book because she came to me and said, "It's time for you to fulfill that purpose. Now let everyone hear your cry."

Also dedicated to my family who has always been there for me, from my mother to both of my fathers, sisters and brothers, my aunties and uncles, my nieces and nephews, my wife, father-in-law, mother-in-law, and sisters-in-law.

See, all these people never gave up on me even though I showed my ass to them. They never turn their backs on me; some even stuck up for me. I love you all, and thank you for pushing me to put these on paper.

Contents

Acknowledgments

I want to acknowledge those who helped me get to this point—to publish this book—first and foremost, my brother Terrance Mitchell, who helped me with my poems.

I want to thank Dr. Darryl L. Claybon who, when I first met him at Strayer University, pushed me to my full potential. Also when I asked him to look over my book, with no hesitation, he said he would. Thank you.

Also I would like to acknowledge this woman because when I was in school at Strayer University, she took interest in me and looked after me during hard times to good times. I was able to talk to her about anything. She even helped me out with some hard decisions in my life. Professor Stephanie Phillips.

I also would like to acknowledge someone who is very special to me. This woman, no matter what I put her through back in the day, was right there making sure I ate. And when I did get myself in a bind, she was right there paying for a lawyer or helping me find my car. Thank you, Nina Olden.

Also thanks to Mrs. Julie Sheppard, who gave me this opportunity to even publish this book. She called me monthly just to check on me and see the status of my book. Thanks to everyone who had a hand in this process to get this book out.

I want everyone to know, this is just the beginning; my next two books will be nonfiction books but a little of the truth also. So look out for them.

Introduction

I named my book *A Father's Cry* because I wanted to let everyone know my fears but, at the same time, what a father like myself has been through that some can't see as a Black father or White. As we walk through life, we can't tell or talk to anyone who would really understand or listen to a man's issues, dealing with babies' mothers, and the drama. Basically who really cares?

I'd been on top, and also thought I was better than some, but God broke me all the way down. He took my family—kids, fathers, mother, brothers, and sisters—took the things that were important to me. I even went to prison. I felt abandoned by everyone.

As these things were going on in my life, I did give up, but my family and new family grabbed me by the hand and pulled me out of the hell that I was going through. I went back to school and received my master's degree in human resources in 2021. So God never gave up on me even though I had given up on myself.

A Father's Cry is my way of telling my dad Michael Ray Burse Sr., that I feel his pain. He asked me as a kid to let him cut my hair, and I replied, "Well, I must ask my dad first." See, that cut deep. I did not know how deep until I got older. All he ever wanted was to be a part of my life. I cursed him, stole from him, and raised up on him. It took me years to grow up and become a man to really understand the tears he shed, that one day as a father, I would shed those same tears too.

A Father's Cry goes without question to my father John Robert Mitchell Sr., who taught me discipline, love, and how to survive without a woman, from washing clothes to cleaning up a house. He was there, but not there in my life, so I had to grow up fast to take care of my five siblings, including myself.

A Father's Cry is when your oldest son curses you because you are drunk. *A Father's Cry* is how he taught you things no other man could. He showed you that trouble is easy to get in but hard to get out. He showed me the true meaning of friends, that, that word is just that word with no meaning. I have no friends honestly. True friends are and were the band of brothers in the infantry who watched my six.

A Father's Cry is for the mothers who raised boys to becoming men, who taught these men how to treat and respect a woman, who showed you how you do not need friends because you have family, who showed that education is the key.

A Father's Cry is for the mothers who are there for their sons no matter what, after a hard day of work, ensure that child's schoolwork is done, make sure that child gets to basketball, baseball, football, or soccer practice etc., who are there when that child is sick, rain or shine.

I called this book *A Father's Cry* because I love my children, but one of my kids does not have my last name, one of my children says my love is toxic, and the other hates me because of what I showed him as he was growing up, that I cared more about the bottle than his feelings or his mother.

See, I know what I have done in the past, but I try to make my relationship better with my children, but at every corner, it is a roadblock. I am pushed and pushed, each time, away from their hearts. I must look after my health first. Another child gives me all her love, knows when I am sad, depressed, or just having a bad day, and still comes to give me a hug or just to see if I am okay.

A Father's Cry does not make much, but we do our damnedest to ensure all our children are taken care of with love by trying to help with homework just so they feel our presences.

A Father's Cry is for us responsible fathers but not given the credit by mothers, talked down of in front of our children.

A Father's Cry is showing everyone that I am not holding anything back anymore!

A Father's Cry is all the tears I have endured over the years. *A Father's Cry* is for my kids to hear my tears, to show my children, real men do cry and sometimes in silence because we do not want to answer the hard question, "Why are you crying, Dad?"

Thank you, who purchased this book. More to come, from Michael Ray Burse Jr.

A Drunken Expression

Don't think for a second that I'm crawling back. No one ever said drunken expression was an excuse to beg for your reaction. Instead, imagine me relaxing in a swimming pool with a barstool, six drinks, and a floating raft to keep me afloat among your continued lies, accusations, and distraction, to forget it ever happened. I see through your diversions; I've been through this before. I've drunk through depression and awoke on the first floor.

It sucks in the conception that I ask forgiveness in the rejection of once calling you mine when I had to share you with another man. You said you loved me or cared for me, but those were lies because the first time you were given a chance, your back was turned on me. But I kept moving on with a smile on my face because I will never allow you the satisfaction of me being vulnerable to the bullshit you speak. All I saw was greed of you having us both, but him finding out the truth, I was freed from your betrayal, and my eyes were opened to the fact of me falling in love with the potential of us but not the potential of you.

Resentful I may be, maybe because the idea of our love was more false than my hopes of us progressing past first base. It's amazing to see how you reacted when I know this reality is no more than an inception you attempted to create. You halted our next step in order to tell him I was a mistake. How could you make me out to be this disgrace? An elegance is all I remember, the one I fell for, the one I could take to forever.

Forever is now no more, happiness is no more, love is no more, loyalty to you is no more, and with us being done, there's no point in you calling my phone. If you die, I wouldn't attend your funeral, so it's safe to say, you aren't even in the friend zone.

Cry's Unheard

Broken is what you hear time after time, broken heart time after
Time, broken dreams accomplishing goal after goal, but no
One is there to see these accomplishments. Broken
Father not able to be close to all his children because
Of the women he chose. Broken father because his
Children won't let him in. Broken barrel after barrel and
No way around them or to avoid them. Broken
Father because he wasn't able to see a child born. Broken
Father because his child doesn't have his last name.
Broken
Broken father children hated because he's with a child
Who loves and cares for him, whom he loves so much.
Broken daughter is jealous of younger sister because
She's with him daily, and she feels left out. Broken oldest son
Pushing up on Dad because he feels his father did his mother
Wrong.
Broken
Broken father apologizes after apology, but nothing
Is heard. Broken, it took the death of a sister
For son to come around and actually enjoy his father.
Broken
Broken daughter dealing with depression, blaming
The father, but no one stands up for him. Broken
Father feels the child's pain and blames himself.
Broken father worries that daughter will get
The thoughts of suicide like her father.
Broken

Broken father not included in knowing about things
Dealing with children, from school to daughter going
To hospital and staying for a week.
Broken
Father trying to get visits, conversation, birthdays with
Youngest son, got nothing, child never there, just
Trying to be that best father with his child but can't.
Broken
Do you know how it feels, no matter what you do or
Doing the right thing to show your children,
You mean well and want the best for them, but
Every effort given, it's rejected by all? Do you know
How it feels because you moved on with your life
But still putting effort to be involved with your children
But no change, rejection after rejection?
Broken
Do you know how it feels to put your heart and feelings
In your youngest child because you've been there
Since day one with her and be blamed for not
Caring for the other children?
Do you know how it feels to hear your oldest daughter say,
"I know you. I am always going to be your
Daughter. No shit, Sherlock, you're down there
With her or them, what about me?"
Do you know how it feels wanting to be there
for her, but you can't reach her?
Do you know how it feels that oldest daughter won't return
Your phone calls nor text?
Broken
Do you know how it feels your daughter feels a certain type,
Away from you because you're with her youngest sister?
Do you know how it feels to let down your children
On birthdays, and that child has the most confidence in
You, and you let her down!
Broken

Broken is broken, is broken,
But what comes after you've been broken all the way down?
There's no more room to be broken.
Broken!

Worry

Worry is a fear given, earned so much to be let down
By worry, of fear that my number one cheated
or been tempted by another man.
I gave my heart no matter what fear she had,
From the drinking to the depression, to the
suicidal thoughts, jumping out of a car,
To not be held at night, to the loss of my sister
and not be consoled by the one I
Love the most, you. So that fear or worry of losing you is there.
When you're not telling me what's on your
mind, that worry became real.
A feeling comes to pass, love only lasts as
long as the other one is in it too.
Time ticks and ticks, but it passes over time.
Feelings last over time, but your
Worries never passes. Relationships are
built on honesty, care, love, trust,
And communication, solely on what the two
really want, built truly on dreams.
Worry sets and kills it all. That season is
gone forever because of that worry.
That one was tempted or cheated. Just tell the truth,
and be free, for that worry goes to pass, and just
Maybe, you could move forward. The thing is, it's more just
two living this dream. It's a child who cares and loves.
So why should she worry if her dad would be here or
if Momma cheated or be tempted by another?
See, worry carries. Worry breaks dreams. Worry breaks
homes. To worry is to worry about the other,

But worry kills everything that two built, so who are you to
say not to worry? Pray is a cure for worry, but to whom
you have that feeling to worry about? That worry
is a thought that is built in your head. That
Worry is that other man giving her that smile you used
to give her. That worry is that other man loving
Her while you were gone. That worry is when you are
down or drunk, and she needs someone else to talk
To. That worry is a *worry no man can control nor
no man will understand. That worry is
Your heart has been broken, just not known yet.
That worry is a worry is she mind or is
She mind or did she run to another man's arms while I was gone.*

So don't say, "Don't worry."
Worry never runs away. You can hold worry
more than you can hold your woman.
Worry comes and goes, but that worry in your household kills.
Worry breaks families. Worry is more stressful than stress itself.
So when you push your lips to say, "Don't
worry," think about what you're saying
Because there is always someone, somewhere, doing that one thing,
Worrying.

L-O-V-E

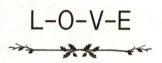

L is for lust or perhaps loneliness.
Either one fuels the mind, the
Impulse is unwavering. Trying to
Distract yourself of the uncertainty,
Built off impeccable chemistry.

O is for opportunity, but choices
Can be so unkind. Must I continue
Living this life without you? I don't
Want to hide you in the shadows, but
Should I break the rule to put an end
To extinction of not having you? Open
Your heart, for our love can be an incredible life you've never had
Before. Look down on your past, for your new man has you up on a
Pedestal.

V is for vulnerability yet the unstable
Ability to be with you. I'm willing to give you my heart and
Die for you. Love can be so blind, but let me
Open your eyes as I intertwine the uniqueness of
Quality time. Bring out the best in me, and put your
Pride aside, and invest in me.

E is for the effort you've shown, that
You care, or could that effort be the
Mask created by your fears? If fear is your enemy, your weapon
I intended to be, put your lips on mine. With our forces

Combined, there's no need to hide. The rigors of
Life may fulfill this emptiness my heart has carried for
So long. Efforts given can liberate my dismal soul
From the unmerciful deception, desperately embraced,
Trying to escape the embodiment of
Love.

Death is no return. Death is that silence that no one hears.
Death is that scream that nobody can hear or help.
Death is that silent cry that no one can wipe.
Death is alone and by yourself.
Death is buried so deep, no matter how hard you yell,
Scratch, bleed, and weep,
Death cannot hear. Always remember,
Death has a begin date, and *death has an end,*
Only on one date.
Make it count for something.

Take Care

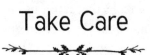

Small, fragile, lovable, she cares about me,
Loves me for who I am, loves
Me mad. Mean or upset,
She still grabs my hand and sits me down on the steps,
Saying, "Daddy, sit, put your arms around me," and we
Just sit, letting me know, "Daddy, I got you.
When you are old, small, fragile, and still
Lovable, always remember, your daughter is
Here through the good and bad."
Ny'lazia, my child.
"I am here, I am here ready to fight you.
I am here, Daddy, the one I can do his nails and lips
I'm here, Daddy.
I will take care of you."

Alone

What is alone?
Alone is life when you are born.
Alone is what you wish you were at.
Alone is dreams that never come true.
Alone is wishing for a woman to love you and never comes.
Alone is wishing of a father to come and save you from
the bullies and demons but never shows up.
Alone is from a father you met when you *were* five,
and you told him, "I must ask my dad."
Alone is when you are standing alone, having to
tell your mother about *your* first *conquest*.
Alone is the tears that run down your face when
you are trying to commit suicide.
Alone is when you are screaming, and no one hears you.
Alone is just that, "alone."
You look left, right, up, and down, *and* no
one is around. You are alone.
Alone is the life that you live.
Alone is dreams *that you kill for.*
Alone is looking for that wife whom you have, but she says no.
Alone is that wife you don't want but you settle for anyway.
Alone is something you can give *but no one can take away.*
Alone is just that, "alone."
Alone is a child who hates you so much 'cause of the mother.
Alone is when you know a child is yours, but you can't be
there because you will mess up his *mother's* money.
Alone is when a child loves you so much but
can't give the other two what she have.
Alone is a dream of telling the truth.

Alone is being *an* ass that every woman told you are.
Alone is when you have kids, and that woman kills
and kills with a kiss, saying, "I love you."
Alone is love that no one understands.
Alone is alone, so where are you alone?
I am here by myself wishing for my kids,
standing alone. Alone is alone.
Alone is when a child gives all her love day in and day out.
Alone is when a child is pushing your buttons
just to make sure you're still on your feet.
Alone is a child who says, "Daddy," daily and mean it.
Alone is the love a child gives that you
cannot get from your other three.
Alone is when she is there standing alone,
pushing her dad to keep pushing.
Alone is a child saying, "Daddy, play with me."
Alone is a child saying, "Daddy, I'm here
for you no matter who's not."
Alone is a child wishing her daddy get over the
heartbreak and pain of the kids he loves so much.
Alone is wishing my dad just see me, the child
that is right here in front of him!
Alone is not the man who raised me because I am right here
Wishing for this woman to love me, wishing
for this woman to have my child,
Wishing for a dream *that you can't give.*
So tell me, am I alone or just standing by myself?
Alone...
Crying is his fear, failure is his fear, fear
of being a bad father is his fear,
Being alone is his fear, but the question I
have really, is my father afraid
Of being alone, or just being loved by one instead of all?
Why does he think he
Stands alone!

I'm here standing right next to you; you're not alone.
Just open your eyes,
And see me.
Alone you will never be. Alone closed the doors on you.
I am here with you, for and always together.
Alone shut down because I have you.
You are loved, so tell alone, "Bye."
Alone can't see you because you are me.
Father, my daddy, my lifeline of love. So alone, go away.
This man is loved.

Last Name

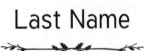

A certain woman can never feel my pain.
You gave my child your husband's last name.
You say, "Look at the gain, you don't have to pay."
You just robbed me, time from a child that's mine.
I don't give shit about him paying; I want my child
To have my last name.
We planned our son. I asked for a DNA just to be a part of his life,
His dreams, wanting to give him that
same love I give my other three
Kids,
But you robbed me of that last name.
You thought Mccain was better than Burse.
I be damned.
I want birthdays, want to take him to school, talk about girls
And dreams, so why be so cruel for check, because you walked out
On me?
So you say, to pay me back, you steal my child's last name?
You afraid to tell him the truth that his father is right here,
And he is a Burse, and not a Mccain?
To some, a last name doesn't mean anything,
But my last name
Means he can be a part of me and know his true family.
Burse, not Mccain.
So tell me, why rob my son his last name?
So let's stop all the BS, and tell him he is not a Mccain,
And give him the rightful
Last name.

Forever Living in Vain

Tell me what you hear. Pain, tears, and the constant fear of being
alone? So is that living in pain or just life of every man fearing to be
a man, a father's constant knocking at the door asking his children
to let him in? Is it the pain, tears, or the constant dreams that
Make you think you're failing as a father, brother,
uncle, cousin, or a future husband?
Tell me what you hear. Pain, tears, or that
constant thought forever living in vain?
Is it that pain knocking at the door, saying, "Let me in.
You will never let me go"? Is it the pain, the tears, or
just lust of living in vain, having one foot in the grave,
screaming, *"Don't leave or close that casket on me!"*
Screaming loud as you can, but no one hears you? Is it
that constant fear of failing as a father, constant knocking
at children's door, asking them to let you in?
Tell me what you hear. Pain, tears? Do you hear that
Constant love from a child who is there with you daily?
Do you hear the tears of that child, saying, "Daddy,
I got you no matter what. I'll be there for you until your
Last days"?
Tell me what you hear. Pain, fear, or just life or the lifestyle
You used to live that's why the constant thought of living
In vain?
Tell me what you hear. The pain, tears of a man doing
His damnedest to ensure his last name is heard? Is it the pain,
Tears, loss of a sister, visiting at her grave and talking
To her for advice? Is it the pain, tears of that constant
Fear, *I'm going to die alone, and no one hears my screams?*
Is it the pain, tears of life's ups and downs, the constant
Life living in vain?

Tell me what you hear. Is it the pain, fear of a child who doesn't
Know his true last name? Is it the fear or tears of a child who
Lost precious time from his father?
Is it the pain, tears, fear that son will know where he came
From? Is it the pain, tears, hope that one day his child,
A son, understands that his last name is Burse, that his
Father named him?
This is the constant fear, pain that no man wants to hear,
That his name or his relationship is being erased from a
child of his whom he haven't even met yet in person.
This is how you live in fear, this is how pain gives in,
This is how love is taken, this is how living in vain
Comes to you.
So tell me now, can you hear my screams? I just want to
Be the best father ever in a painful life
Of tears and fears of
Life living in vain.

Just a Thought

It never fails to cut deeper, the wound healed with the lies my mind is hesitantly willing to tell itself. Do you love someone so much that you are willing to watch them be happy with someone else? I do not need the sweet talk or the minor abrasions of you inconsistently not wanting to be with me, cutting me once to the depths of my soul upon return. You treat me as if my pure intentions are an hors d'oeuvre, use me, and then your excuse is that you couldn't discern if my position in what we created was an attempt to appease an itch or to place a ring on that four for our future to flourish. As we flourish, we base the foundation of our relationship on communication and not worry about stressful thoughts of our significant other surreptitiously surrendering to the temptation of someone who doesn't give you the satisfaction or motivation to continue to build what we began. Remember the first moment that faint glimpse of my silhouette caused your heart to skip a beat. Apart from obvious thoughts of comparison to him, you and I both know his deepest form of affection fails in comparison to me placing a kiss upon your cheek. Even if periodically our future seemed bleak, I would dive into the fires of desire to save you from thinking our moments of passion we shared were no more than fully body massage and a two-hour retreat.

Question

Why does my name mean so much?
What would your name leave?

(Best father ever)

(How can I make history books?)
BoSina 2001
Iraq 2004–2005
Iraq 2006–2008
But no mark!

What do you see when you look at me?
How do I get there?
That dash on the tombstone in between, what does it really mean?
Yes, it shows the dates of my life, but that
in between, will anyone ever
Notice the things I did in between?
Will they talk about my military career?
Will they talk about my mistakes I made?
Will they say good or bad things about me?
What will be the mark for me before my death?
Will my children come see me when I'm on my last breath?
Who will be near me or hold my hand before I go?
That dash, will it tell everything about me?
What will be the mark for me to leave?

Beaten

Headstrong, stubborn, boring,
Sexual, mean, and an ass.
Never wore chains, never been to Africa.
Beaten is going to Iraq, being shot,
Seeing friends get hurt and die.
Beaten is thinking you are the cause of your parents
Divorcing. Beaten is when you could share your
First with your dad but had to share it with your mother.
Beaten is when you take responsibility of five other kids.
Beaten is when you learn the meaning of friends. Beaten
Is when you take on death at the age of
thirty-nine. Beaten is when you
Marry the wrong women and have kids.
Beaten is when she brainwashed the kids against you.
Beaten is when you are giving a child so much love,
And she gives it back. Beaten is when you defend this child from
Your other two, and she hates you for it.
Beaten is beaten, no matter how it is or seem.
Believe when I say this, I have taken a beating.
When given the correct beating,
That beating after beating, that man
That is came too. So no
More beating.

History

All I do is dream, all I do is wish on a star, and dream some more.
I give and give, then I take and take, but
dreams come true most of the
Time, wishes would become true most of
the time. Bottom line is, I am
Already in the history books with the Iraq
war; I want more. I want my
Name in history books that you cannot
take away. A dream that cannot
Be missed and a wish that cannot be sought.
I want the name Burse to live
Forever in a way other than my children.
I want my name to live in life.
Every time you turn a page in the history
book, and you go to B (Burse),
You'll find me, the man who broke barrels,
a man of dreams of a man of
Stars.
See, I believe Iraq made me a bachelor's
degree, gave me a chance, and
A master's degree gave me more. I gave my kids my last name,
Gave them a dream, gave them a wish, showed them how to work
For what they do. Now look at my nonpicking-cotton hands, look
At my brown eyes, look at the Black man
you cannot make nor break,
Look at this Black as a threat like you do all Black men whom you
Sought as a threat, Martin Luther King, Malcom X, Huey Newton,
Then soon it will be me, Michael Burse Jr.
See, those stars and dreams we seek, it
goes more than basketball and

football. I'd rather be in a book, which some cannot read and some
Can. Main thing, you must pick one up
to seek me. The main thing is
This, you run from books because books
tell you the truth of a Black man
and what we built. I have not built shit,
but believe when I say this, I
built a dream, I built a wish, and everything I write and say, that star
makes it come true because no one can stop me. I believe in myself
because *my* children believe in this *Black man*. I am that star you
wish upon, and my daughter Ny'lazia will
tell you, "My daddy is all that.
My daddy showed me how to run, showed me my education
Is everything. My daddy showed me how
to wash dishes, clean, and cook.
My dad showed me, a man is nothing
without his word, and if he hits a
Woman, he is not even shit more. But I do know that, for this *Black*
man showed me how to shoot and told me, if I must call him,
I had no worries because your ass is grass. Now wish upon a star
Because that star is fucked. This Black man is not coming to ask
Questions about your dreams of me, and you just went to shit.
History is what he seeks, and dreams are what he takes. I love my
Dad. Everything he does for me, I will do for him. Me and my dad,
We seek the same history, and please believe, my dad is halfway
There. He reads and reads and teaches. Have you heard of Henrietta
Lacks, an African American who was diagnosed
with cervical cancer at John
Hopkins Hospital, and the *White* surgeons
took tissue samples of her
tumor without her permission or her
knowledge? Henrietta's cells were the
line of human cells to live outside of the
human body in culture. Her
cells are what nationwide goes off of today
for cancer. Also Wall Street

came from where? Before it was Wall Street, it was *Black Wall Street*, which was burned down by jealous White folks! Please understand, I am only three years old. I spend a lot of time with this Black man. We have fun together; you wouldn't think that because of the Negativity you hear about a Black man. This Black man, my father, Michael Ray Burse Jr., is present every day, from schoolwork, holidays, Birthdays, and even more. I have a brother, Michael III, and an older Sister, Zy'Ciaha. He balances us; we are treated all the same. I wish upon a star, and hopefully one day, my dad's dreams come True. My dad is hurt all the time, and all he talks about is my brother and Sister. How he wishes upon a star, how he dreams that they will come And stay with us. All I can give him is a kiss and hug and keep him Busy. This Black man I know, my dad, he never shows it, but he hurts. Help me get him up there. My dad is a *great man. He* has taught Me a lot. I just wish my sister and brother could see him as I see him. History is already written for my fallen star, my dad, Michael Burse.

Dear Past

I want to thank you for allowing me to prove
to everyone that I'm different. This
Isn't a complaint session; hell, I just wanna vent
sometimes. I wonder, *Am I a product*
Of my environment? No resentment on my life
struggles or even where I'm from,
Put yourself in my shoes to understand what
I had to adapt to in life to overcome.
At a young age, my life was in shambles, boy,
what a mess. In life, you either prepare
For failure or prepare for success. I talked to
Satan a few hours ago; he told me
About my placement within society and how
far I should go to manipulate it,
All the way until shade turns to darkness on a
road, dividing, departing clothed. The
Root of all controversy, my presence, a courtesy
to the bold, standing in the middle,
Staring into your eyes as blatant as time's cloak.
You see, I am more simple than
Man, a pivotal part of the plan to incite fear
and invoke uncertainty and pride. You
Decide if your heart can bare the same ember
as coal. He told me about restraint
And sadness, how to replace them with hope
false enough to allow me to shape
Beliefs, turning a blessing into tragedy. The
reality is, the beginning of my
Existence goes back to when forward time
first became you, the past. He spoke

Those words, and in that moment, I was
created too. I am none other color, and
Treated as such, crossed burning in efforts
to deter me from my rights when I
Was created before you took your first breath.

Family Promise

Michael Ray Burse Jr., Nikia Quinshonda Woodberry,
Ny'lazia Shynte'le Woodberry.
We will forever be one family that *no* man can
Tear apart. Through the thickness of the night and
The brightness of the day, we will forever be a part
Of each other's life till the day the Lord calls us
Home.
Swear amen!
A family promise is what she gave me. You cannot see
What she did, but she promised me something that most
People could not give me, not the first wife
nor the second nor the third.
"I gave him something, promised
A child. I gave him me. I gave him a dream of hope.
I gave him more than lust. I gave him support.
A family promise, I'll give him hell, keep him on his toes.
Family promise is not all good nor bad, but like always,
I'm there. I might get mad, but at the end of the day,
Before we rest, I don't take our negative in our bedroom.
I might curse, hate him today, but at night,
When it's time to rest, that promise I gave him comes
To play.
He cleans, he cooks, he fuss, and he fights depression
And PTSD, but this man, Michael, I love dearly. This is why
This family promise, I will never break again.

Yes, I might have sent another man a picture instead of him,
But I realized this man is a true man because he didn't
Walk away from me! He fussed, he cursed, and didn't
Talk to me, but he loved our child and loved me.
That family promise, he has never broken. So
Say what you want; I love him.
Family promise, that's him."

Older, Colder, and Bolder

Thick thighs, pretty smile is what I see. Can I approach you, or can
I just tell what I want? I want to taste the pussy, see if you
Can suck it good, make my toes curl, or make me nut within five.
Older, colder, and much bolder
Tell you how I want it, to tell you how to give it to me!
Want to fuck you in the ass and do not have to call after
Until I want some more.
Big breasts, medium, it does matter, as long
as I can touch them, lick them,
Tease them. See, older, colder, and bolder, they tell you how it is.
No reading between the lines, no promises,
no comments, just a nice fuck,
A good nut is what she wants.
Nasty at times, but freaky all the time.
Let me put my tongue in your butt; suck my dick until I nut.
Let me push it to the back of your throat until I am tired.
Let me stand up in the pussy until the morning sun comes.
See, older, colder, and bolder, she tells me how it is,
Even says when no other questions asked.
Older, colder, and bolder, this is a Black woman I see in my dreams.

Honeycomb

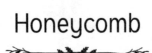

There was a honeycomb that stood alone among the dying flowers and darkened leaves. The fluid deep inside—golden, sweet—dripped ever so slowly, never more than a steam. He saw this and imagined what it would be like to stop and drink. Peculiar for these darkened leaves to conceal a treasure so unique, death holding onto life's flavorful peak. He approached closer in hopes of testing what existed just out of his reach, only to see that the glimmer among the darkness was a priceless trail toward deceit. Through the honey was a sign that warned of trespassing. He turned and saw a man aiming, as he felt beestings yet buzzing.

Cut Deep

It never fails to cut deeper, the wound healed
with lies my mind is hesitantly
Willing to tell it self. Do you love someone so
much you are willing to watch them
Happy with someone else. I don't need sweet
talk or the minor abrasion of
Inconsistently not wanting to be with me, cut
me once to the depths of my soul
Upon no return. You treat me as if my pure
intention are an hor's d'oeuvre, use me
And then your excuses is that you couldn't
discern, if my position in what we
Created was attempt to appease as itch or to
place a ring on that four our future to
Flourish we base the foundation of our
relationship on communication and not
Worry about the stressful thoughts of our
significant other surreptitiously
Surrendering to the temptation of someone
who doesn't give you satisfaction
Or motivation to continue to build what
began. Remember the first moment
That faint glimpse of my silhouette caused
your heart to skip a beat, apart from

Obvious thoughts of comparison to him, you
and I both know his deepest form
Affection pails in comparison to me placing
a kiss upon your cheek, Even if
Periodically our future seemed bleak, I would
dive into the fires of desire to save
You from thinking our moments of passion
we shared were no more than full
Body message and a two hour retreat.

Spoken Words

I remember the first words spoken to me
like it was a script from a movie.
From the confident walk to your sexy talk, I
know when you are in the room. Since
The day I laid eyes on you, things wouldn't be
the same as you gaze into my eyes.
Heart racing, the attraction stimulates my brain.
I mean, you could make the blind see
if you've just walked past them. Your
Physique is like a diamond among ashes.
See, you are vividly attractive. You
Would never be lost at sea. Your elegance
would be too apparent. Your voice is
Like that calming waterfall that roars with
strength, yet is gentle enough for
Me to see my reflection. You show me how
I need to improve when my water
Begins to look stagnant. My heart beats
visually, can't you see, especially when
You walk so enticing? My soul unwinds
when words are more like actions.
Behold, none other similar, your uniqueness is
peculiar. Take hold of this moment;
It may last forever. You are my savior at times;
I know that if I hung by a rope, you
Would cut me down from depression's strangle.
I am never alone in battle. You are
A queen, but you'd get your crown bloody to
help protect our castle. Kind and

Sweet, you are a flavor I long to taste and
embrace, like that stolen bite of food
Before dinner. How clever, whenever I need
you, you are there, absent of questions,
Only answers.

Unknown Depths

In the unknown depth of life, I have
welcomed you in my heart with no
Reputes of you shattering it if doubt
should ever creep in your mind.
Through the interaction with society, I
couldn't imagine thinking love
Was real. Love is blind, or is it only for
those who truly wish to see in
Someone or the fear of just being alone and having to settle? When
Hearing the dreaded three, "I love you,"
questions populate my head.
Do you love yourself? Do you know your worth? Is love learned?
Would you have love or peace? Can you
have both? "For God so loved
The world, that he gave his only son that
whosoever believes in him will
Not perish but have everlasting life." If you fear love, how can you
Experience fully what is abundant and worthy of cherishing? Doubt
Is a drug, but living sober is evermore refreshing than the shameful
Realization that doubt could leave you embarrassed, especially if
Doubt is painted on the one's worth of
trust, love, and marriage. Love is
Vivid. With care in your visual, pain
becomes invisible. Because if love
Is worth fighting for, the war is not a
battle. To love yourself is to love
Others. If we love others as we love ourselves,
would there not be peace
Instead of streets riddled with pieces of
broken hearts that cause others

To stumble, emotional roadkill, the
heartless preying on the meek? If
Love was apart from peace, that would
mean, with the shining of light
And eyes that perceive, no one would see.

What Happens When False Memory Seduces Desire?

What happens when false memory seduces desire? A
trauma that tightens the noose that suffocated
Reality, the funeral of fantasy's facade. The numerous
careless impulses combine, forming an entity
That rages and draws strength from the lies. Apart from
the truth that lies beneath the fruitful glimpses
Of a pleasant demise there, a reason why to express
who you truly are is ignorantly unwise.
Vulnerability is suicide. No soul is inclined to portray
what they meant to hide, especially if what is
Longed for is farther from near what others aspire to
be. Woe is me. Honestly, if ever with breath, life
Was ever meant for me, be it unto me, a death that
I am elated to never see. For be it from me, an
Existence that fails to compare to the rain that
showers down and drowns me. Straining for air,
Searching for what to believe, what actually happened,
the arousal of speech that flows like blood,
Which drips like tears profusely. I am two me, I am
but he, so broken that I appear newly complete.
Abstract, comforting to image the countless moments
that never transpired but warm my heart like
Our wedding. The lies that blanket my subconscious
while dreaming, a time where tomorrow should
Never despise me, with truth that shatters my wish for
her and me. What happens when false memory
Seduces desire? Her and me. A traumatic love story.

Twisted Tongue

You speak the truth it hurts.
But be true.
You are a better man now than you were before.
Kids hate you, but who cares?
Twisted tongue
You want a house, but your woman will not let you lead.
Your spirit will not let you move forward. LOL.
Shit, you will not even get married. Push back, push back.
Twisted tongue
Who cares you gave the earnest money up and lied about,
But let us go back though.
Father says you like him coldhearted. You
Send another man a text and a picture your man asked for.
The man you love.
This man takes care of his child, his lifeline, but you cannot trust
Him to take care of a bill.
A twisted tongue will tell you.
Your daughter knows her daddy more than she knows you,
Her own mother.
LOL
I ask you what I mean to you.
Silence like death,
What are you looking for out of me?
Do you trust me, or you only trust me with
child you are not around for?
Twisted tongue
You do not give a shit about me.
Less sex, got to get you high just to get the freaky side out.
I am the nigga who brings everything out of you, but you
Want to marry him.

I'm not the nigga you really want; I am just time.
Twisted tongue
I am the guy you stood up for my sister-in-law.
When she called, crying naked,
Busted a nigga with a bottle, and he went to get his
Neighbors, saying, "You're not from the streets.
Always remember, I am the original hot boy from 601.
Cops could not fuck with me."
Twisted tongue
I'm the brother-in-law who loves you dearly.
Cannot accept a nigga calling you a bitch or a hoe.
I am not that guy who expects everything you say.
Twisted tongue
I know you for who you are. I know your sister for
Who she is, I know your sister for her,
I don't have friends, but I have a sister-in-law who loves me
For who I am,
That man who will come no matter what my sister says.
Rikia/Keke
I know both can do better, but you'd rather settle for less.
LOL
Not funny, those niggas are not shit without y'all.
Your sister sees a real man, but her eyes are closed.
She just doesn't know, if you could have me, you would run with it.
Now it is a price for me.
I am taking everything for now on
Hearts
Twisted tongue
Can you handle me?

Queen

In your arms is where I want to be, a safe haven,
a happy place for you and for me.
You help take my pain away. You smile so big,
it brightens up the day. No faking,
Just genuine true feelings. Operating on different
frequency when you are next to
Me. Energies combine because we both are
on the same time. A true queen
You are, nothing less. You inspire me to be
my best. Lovemaking, nothing short
Of amazing, taking my body to different
elevations. Whatever you want, baby,
I'm yours for the taking. Catering to you as a
man is what I supposed to do. Nothing
More I want but build, secure, bless, grow,
and love my future with you.

To Myself

Can I be honest with you? A part of me still
desires her visual, ever present before
Me and not just in pictures. I miss her voice
through the silent whisper of written
Poetry, aimed at my heart sexually. I want to
taste her clitoris, rub her sensually,
Kiss her neck while we vibe to music, and drink
from the vineyards. I just want to be
Intimate, hold her in my arms, and wipe her
tears while she reads to me her deepest
Feelings, the ones she hides from herself so
that she can appear confident. I miss
Hearing her tell me she loves me. Though never
spoken, the veins that connect to
My arteries feel it. I just hope she can feel this.
The strings of my heart torn, and I
Only want her to mend them. An apple from
her orchard, I wonder would she like it
If I bite into it. Or maybe I should just quit,
getting high off of what ifs and lost
Memories. A part, never whole or adjacent.
We started then rolled off that cliff,
Down it, never seemed to stop it, left us so
weightless and astonished, debating
If we were really honest. I just couldn't believe
that time would cause so much
Destruction through the purely diluted
feelings of "love" that we drowned in.
Dumbfounded. I just need to sink into her
one time; it wouldn't help. But if

We ever saw each other again, could we
speak and not touch each other's
Subconscious? You know I'm telling truth,
so stop hiding it, and let her move
On.

Educated but No Fool

See, I walk around with my head held high, but I hurt inside.
Most people see me, but I feel at times, I am just passing time.
You see a Black man, but you judge me just like the rest.
Not knowing I served in the military, not
knowing I have a bachelor's
Degree in criminal justice—but like always, typical Black man—
Not knowing I have a master's degree in human resources.
Humm…I got your attention now. See,
this Black man is educated but
No fool. The question is still, what do you see?
See, I'm a real Black man who takes care of all his kids. See, I'm
A Black man; when I give my love, I give
it my all. See, I am a Black man
Who has fought just like any, but fuck with
my kids, you will see a Black
Man, you did not want to see. See, in
American skin, a child was killed, and
The twisted was even the father who pulled
the trigger, and they did not kill the
Man. See, this Black man would make sure
he died and the partner with him.
See, I love my life but will give it up for my kids.
Educated but no fool.
See, I am a proud Black man who loves
Black women, would protect any
No matter the color of their skin.
See, what if I told you I had a felony; first
thing you would think of is for drugs,
Rape. None of the above. Someone spit in my face, but like always.

The man, the aggressor, and the woman I was
with never came to my aid. Three
Versus one. But since having a military background
and in a racist state, I had no chance.
Educated but no fool.
See, that does not stop me from pushing
myself. I see life just as any there is, no
Limit and all possibility of what is next for me.
So when you look at me, do not judge me; ask
me or give me the benefit of the doubt.
'Cause I do not judge you, not my place.
But believe this, all Black men are not the same.
This Black man is educated, lovable, faithful,
responsible, and I take care of
My kids. No one takes care of me; I hold my own.
Always remember, educated and honest and no fool!

Who Are You Trying to Please?

Beaten for trying to save her son for being a momma's boy.
Beaten for working late. Beaten for the tears of
A son. Beaten for loving his mother than his father, can't walk away.
Who are you trying to please?
Afraid of being alone, afraid of sleeping alone! You're not a man. You
are someone I can't believe is a man whom I cheated with, thinking
you were more than what you are. You are not the him! I wish you were
like the man I dream of, the man I dream about, the man I lust about,
the man for me. I wish you were like the man my sister have. I want
my sister's man, a real man. I want a man like my father, a supportive
man who knows how to take care of a home, take care of kids.
Who are you trying to please?
My kids love their uncle; he listens. He does things with them this
man can't do. I can talk to him about him, and he doesn't judge me,
But my man will call out my name and tell me to go sleep with
another man. Damn, why am I trying to please this man?
A man who respects me, I want the man my father was when he was
young, who can ask for my hand. I want the man like my brother-
in-law; no matter the demons he have, he is his own man who had
something before me, not jealous. I had lived before him. I lived.
Save me from myself. I am young trying to live life like my sister, but it's
not working. I feel sad, alone, wishing on a dream, wishing my brother-
in-law will save me; he showed me how a man is supposed to be.
So who am I trying to please?
I can't save myself, so how can I save anyone else?
I'm in love with a woman and a child but believe she's just passing time.
So who am I trying to please?
I've been with a child since she really came home. I'm daddy. I am
momma. I teach her good and bad. Grandparents want her, but
it's a time limit before they call the auntie. Writing tells it all.

My oldest child hates my daughter for being there for
me, there for her dad, got me to where I need to be. You
hare her 'cause I was deployed when the TV fell on you,
and they see at your brother before they see at you.
You won't give your dad or father a chance, so
tell me, who are you trying to please?
My father is one of the most dangerous man in the world. He plays
with me, he does everything with me, and he even talks about my
brothers and sister to me. Mmmmm…piss him off or do something to
us, you will really see him, my daddy. But he loves us, believe that.
So who are you trying to please?
I have what I want; I have a father who shows me everything.
I don't have a father who is there all the
time. I know it's what I am told.
I used to believe in my father, but then he left my mother.
So who are you trying to please?

I'm not trying to please anyone. I just want to make my father happy, showing him I listen to everything he taught me, and I listen. But at the same time, I know my father, the man who raised me, will die alone, and I will be right there no matter if my brothers or sister will be there. I will be there for this old man. I love this man. Who was he trying to please? No one but himself. You want to know a real man? His name is Michael Ray Burse Jr., my father. So when you read this poem, he pleased me, my sister and brother, my aunties, and mother. He doesn't have to please no one, but he did please me.

Please everyone know help me right this poems. I put myself in everyone's shoes, of those whom I wrote about in this poem. Some of these poems are fictional. My child is only three years old. There's no feelings for the auntie or hard feelings for any grandparents because I can count on them more than anything. Wanted to just put that out there.

Disgruntled Woman

Hurt, bitter woman uses your kids against you.
Text message after text cut you down.
She is letting your children disrespect the man who was there through
    birth,
Taught them how to say words, played with, went to school plays,
    no credit though.

Disgruntled woman
She just wants and wants. I need this. I need that.
You give and give, then you come across a good woman who teaches
    you how to
Love, shows you support, but
in your head, even though you do a lot, you feel
You failed as a father.

Disgruntled woman
Complaint after complaint, you say your children blame you for not
    being there.
Complaint after complaint, you say I am wrong for moving on with
    my life.
Complaint after complaint, say you have two kids who are not yours.

Disgruntled woman
You walked away not telling both.
Grew out of each, just saying, "Daddy cheated," makes you look
    good.
"Daddy got the money," but you only tell the kids to call only when
    it comes
To money.

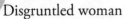

Disgruntled woman
Let your child talk over the phone but will not give him his father's
    last name.
A check is better than a father's love, and the man paying is wrong
    unless
He knew something I do not. A disgruntled woman will not tell.
Milk it until the end,
Disgruntled woman.

Blame Me

Children, blame me for not being there day in day out. Blame me
    for deployments,
missing your first steps or speak your first words. Blame me for cheat-
    ing on your
mother. Blame me for showing you life, a lifestyle, but not preparing
    you for being
alone. Blame me because you do not have my last name. Blame me
    for letting
another man pay child support. Blame me for not being there on
    your first day of school.
Blame me for not telling you about girls or boys. Blame me for not
    showing you the
love I show the other three and you do not get. Blame me because I
    am and
became a man. Blame me for caring about my career than showing
    love. Blame me for
everything your mother said about me. Blame me for the hurt and
    the pain you
feel. Blame me 'cause all I am, and you taught is money. Blame me
    because I
have not met you in person yet. Blame me.

I want to let my children know I love them all. I am a good father.
    All I ask is, give
me a chance to show it so you'll forgive me because I may not be
    there physically, but love
me, call me, just say, "Hello, Dad," or Father, which you want to call
    me. I'm your
father, and my love is endless. Love you always.

Blame me.

Death Is Coming

Death is coming. I see him in my dreams.

I see death every morning in the mirror, looking at my own reflection.

I know death is coming, just don't know when or how or what time,
     but

Death is coming.

Death is that pain hearing your child say love is toxic.

Death is when your try's you at the age of fifteen.

Death is when you go through your woman's phone and the pictures
     you asked for,

And she sent them to another man instead of you.

Death is when your sister is taken before her time.

Death is when you know you are afraid.

Death is when you are in that casket in the

Dark, then put in the ground six feet deep, dirt covering you.

You are screaming, crying, but no one can hear you.

Roses are dropped, tombstone is

placed, name, birth, and death, and what you meant to some.

Death is coming, but death is already here. I smile for you daily, go
     through the

motions, scared to tell your Veterans Affairs counselor the truth.

Death is my face, and I'm screaming, no one hears me, so I cry
     silently and hold

My pain in.

Death is coming.

Lie, Lie, Lie

Tell me you love me but send another man a picture.

Tell me, Daddy, you are coming but never show up.

Tell me, Daddy, when I need you, you'll be right there.

Lie, lie after lie.

Tell me you are thinking of me, but deep inside, you want to be somewhere else.

Tell me you're enjoying my company but wishing you were with him.

Tell me you marry me.

Tell me you give our child my last name.

Lie, lie after lie.

Tell me when I don't have it, you will help me.

Tell me you will never leave and run to another man.

Daddy, tell me, you'll send me a gift on every birthday.

Tell me, Daddy, when Momma's not showing me attention, you will.

Tell me, Daddy, Momma's boyfriend is a better father than you.

Lie, lie after lie.

Tell me, Daddy, where were you when I was getting bullied?

Tell me, Daddy, why Mother tells you last about everything in all things

Including about our health?

Tell me, Daddy, how come my sister gets more love than me and my brother?

Tell me, Daddy, is that my little brother, and why doesn't he have your last name?

Or why haven't you or I met him?

Tell me, Daddy, why do I feel they get more time than me?

Lie, lie after lie.

Tell me this, where are you when I need you?

Where are you for my games, my homework, our birthdays,
    Christmas, and more?
Stop telling me what you do, how you do it, that you're showing up
    on this
Day and don't show up.
Stop the lies after lies.
I know you are a good father, I know you love me,
I know it's a wall there, but if you hit one side, and I hit the others,
And my brothers and sister hit also,
We, together, will break this wall of lies down and be happy.
No more lie, lie after lie.

Believe

If God was Jewish, doesn't that make us all Jewish?
Can you believe it's life after death?
Can you believe that United States is built on all racists' blood?
Can you believe that United States is built on lies?
Can you believe some fathers do it all no matter if they're not with
    the mother of their
Children?
Let me tell you what I believe.
I'm hated by some family,
Loved by many,
Cared by few.
I believe God put me through things to see if I can handle it and to
    see if I will
Denounce him.
I believe my Satan comes for me daily.
I believe my kids hate me but one.
I believe I will be old and alone.
I believe no matter how happy I am, I will never be fully happy.
I believe the woman I love and care so much will break my heart and
    walk
Away.
I believe at the end of the day, only one person really has me.
I believe in him.
Believe.

Fear

Fear is afraid to fail.

Fear is that failure you believe you did with your kids.

Fear is love believing no matter how many times you get married, you will never

Feel just loved by one.

Fear is giving your all for your kids, but they can't see what you do or believe in

You.

Fear is that failure as a father.

Fear is dreams, wishes that are broken, family taken.

Fear is us thinking, hoping that history doesn't repeat itself.

Fear is wanting too much.

Fear is a felon, thinking you can't do nothing no matter

The two degrees you have.

Fear is fear.

Fear is just that, no matter how you cover it up, say it, dress it,

That fear of death and love will always still be right

There in the morning.

It's still just that, your fear!

Reflection

Staring in the mirror, looking for the man I am, but there's no reflec-
tion there,

No care, no love, no dreams, nothing. Where did I go?

I call out to this reflection of mine and say, "Sir, answer me, who are
you?

Where are you? Tell me, reflection, why can't I see anything looking

Back at me?

Reflection, are you rejecting me like my kids? Reflection, are you
rejecting

Me like my wife did twenty years ago when I asked her to marry me?

Reflection, tell me, are you mad at me for daydreaming of another
woman?

Reflection, fucking answer me!

Reflection, tell me what color is my skin.

Reflection, if I knock on this mirror, will you knock back?

Reflection, if I come closer, will you hear me and say something back?

Reflection, tell me what kind of man I am.

Reflection, am I a lovable man?

Reflection, am I a hated man?

Reflection, do I lust over one woman who is not mine but would just
like to see

Her in a way that I see my reflection?

Damn, reflection, answer me!

Reflection, tell me why I have tried multiple times to hurt or kill
myself

But always wake up the next day.

Reflection, what is your plan for me?

Reflection, how come you show me the same darkness I see when I
close my eyes?

Reflection, why is the reaper standing next to me each time I come
to see you?
Reflection, tell me why I am always alone.
Reflection, why do I keep asking you to save me from myself?
Reflection, if I turn the lights on, will I see me, or will I see you, and
will that be the same?"
Reaper asks me the same question,
"Why you are looking at me. Because I am you, and you are me.
Your reflection is my reflection, only you can change what you see
and do.
So stop asking me, your reflection, what I can do for you when you
can
Only do for you."
So, reflection, shake my hand and do what no man can do other than
me and you.
Reflection, now I see me. I wonder when I walk out this door, will
everyone see
Me as I see me, more than what I see in my mirror looking at my
reflection?

There for Him As for Me

As she was there for him, she was there for me. The difference is, he is not a family friend, not kin, not like it was right then when my kin died. She was there for me just as she was there for him. I want but can't have, never crossed that line.

But over time, feelings came real. Worried about what kin would say, look at like this, I never crossed that line even though the feeling was real. See, it's okay though when your kin sleeps or fucks your baby's mother while you're in the next room.

Since I never acted on mine, bottled it up and kept it inside, at least I know I'm real. She was there for you as she was there for me. My kin died, same as yours. The only difference is, brothers are fucking the same girl, not a family friend but kin.

I want but can't have nor never crossed that line. She was there for him as she was there for me. Family wouldn't see you, rather judge you, but not judge the kin who fucked your girlfriend / baby's mother.

Even though we consider each other as friends, tell you things that I don't tell others, she was there for him as she was there for me, not a family friend nor kin, never crossed that line even though the feeling was genuine. All I could do is dream and still have not crossed that line. She was there for him as she was there for me, not a family friend nor kin.

See, you might judge me, but I never crossed that line. I have expressed my feelings to her but never approached her. See, it's some who have it worse than me. Only difference, I write mine on paper instead of doing what I feel. So before you judge, judge your damn selves, and shut the fuck up, that's real.

She was there for him as she was there for me.

I wrote this poem because a certain family member made a statement, saying they do not fuck with me because I made a statement that a certain female was attractive back in the day. Well, bottom line, I never crossed that line, but certain members have, but you bite your tongue with them.

Can't Love

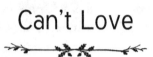

Every ounce of blood in my body, I can show love, care, patience, support, and love, but there's no doubt, knowing if I show it all, I'll be walked on and left alone.

I just can't love.

I can't love 'cause of doubt, and the love I gave was taken advantage of. I told no to marriage, so why not give up on love? Doubt runs through every ounce of my blood. I've given all but taken advantage of. I cared for my own children whom I gave all my love, disrespected, only care is you want me to buy your love.

Doubt runs deep. I can't love. My own told me all I give is toxic love, but a picture tells a thousand words.

I gave my love to another plan, a child I've never met, so how can you give a son love who doesn't even know you? So is that love?

I can't love.

I gave love to her and went to prison because she could stand against her family, knowing they were in the wrong, showed love, lie after lie. You can't even talk to the child whom you know is yours. He can't even have your last name.

I can't love because when asked for a DNA, she says, "You're welcome to, but you will not get one because my ex-husband pays child support for the son that supposed to be yours."

So why love?

I can't love.

Life Changed

My life changed on June 27, 2020, at 5:05 a.m., when every ounce of love drained out of me, afraid to tell my other living brothers and sisters I love them.

Life changed on June 27, 2020, at 5:05 a.m., when I think back and my sister said, "How come you never said you're proud of me or you love me?" See, that day replays in my head day in and day out.

Life changed on June 27, 2020, at 5:05 a.m., when you just talked to your youngest sister who died the same night.

Life changed when you cursed your mother and blamed her for your sister being gone. (But you were hurt and couldn't take it out on anyone else.) Love your mother, Angela Mitchell.

Life changed fighting a husband trying to get your sister's body back to lay her to rest.

Life changed on June 27, 2020, at 5:05 a.m., when your baby sister's in a brown box with just a sheet over her, wondering how she died, or asking, did she die alone?

Life changed when Lasonya Burse died; now I am sharing all my deepest pain with you.

Life changed on June 27, 2020, at 5:05 a.m.

About the Author

Michael R. Burse Jr. was born on October 15, 1981, in Hinesville, Georgia. He was an Army brat birthed by Michael R. Burse Sr. and Angela Mitchell, raised by John Mitchell Sr. Michael is the second to the oldest out of six children. His siblings are Cantina Burse, Lasonya Burse, Shunquishia Mitchell, John Mitchell Jr., and Terrance Mitchell.

He graduated from Orange Park High School, Jacksonville, Florida. He continued his education in the Army and received his associate's degree in criminal law from Texas Technical College in 2007. He also graduated from Strayer University with a bachelor's degree in criminal justice in 2014.

From there, he attended Southern New Hampshire University in 2017 and graduated with a master's degree in human resources in 2021.

Also, his other siblings are Mac Shane Burse, Tavia Burse, and Quinta'sha Mitchell.

He joined the military in 2001 and served in Hawaii 25th Infantry Division, 10th Mountain Division, and 2nd Infantry Division. He was deployed to Iraq three times, twice as an infantry soldier and once as a civilian. He loved military until the day he got out in 2009. He has seen the world and grew up in the military.

He married on March 12, 2021, to a lovely lady named Nikia Q. Woodberry. He has four children—Michael Ray Burse III, Zya'Ciaha Genesis Burse, Micha Mccain, and Ny'Lazia Shyne'ce Woodberry.

CPSIA information can be obtained
at www.ICGtesting.com
Printed in the USA
LVHW040744291222
735979LV00002B/218

9 781639 852208